morning air,
morning light

morning air, morning light

regan noelle smith

regannoellesmith.com

ISBN: 978-1-7376433-0-2

Cover design + art by Zane Miller
Cover flower art by Alex Miller
Illustrations by Regan Noelle Smith

ATTN: SCHOOLS AND BUSINESSES
This book is available at quantity discounts with bulk purchase for educational, business, or sales promotional use. For information, please contact the author and team via regannoellesmith.com.

d e d i c a t i o n

Dedicated to those
who feel as though
they are breaking–
for we are all broken at birth.

But divine espial offered–
aligned before us, above us;
reaching our arms up,
as we extend, our fingers
intermingle with this rich warmth.

All-encompassing grace–
a peace that is sky stretching,
freedom's fluid
further than the ocean's flow,
healing like holy basil–
slowly and softly, but wholly.

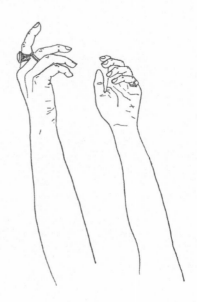

preface

This initial chapter, Nightfall, is composed of poems, depicting my past–delved deep. I urge you to read through the first chapter, but not to seal the pages there. For the promised land, the land of milk and honey, is found within the chapters that follow.

As I wrote out each elapsed era of my life, I noticed that they spilled out of my pen to paper without reservation. Each word revealed more clarity, offering transparency. It brought back memories that I've blocked out. They played like a nebulous, painful parody–a broken cinema reel of concentration.

I revisited these recollections that have been quarantined. With eyes glazed over, these memories were recorded to tangible form. Each word written tore away an unyielding nail from the boards which hid a remote, abandoned door that I had rarely acknowledged. These experiences are raw and honest, evoking emotions that I hadn't endured in years.

It's almost unfathomable that this was at once the present time; I would have never expected my current state to contrast so vastly.

I was able to write these flashbacks of calamity without being overcome with anxiety. This is because I know that there is a God with overruling grace who provides comfort through any situation. Even when the bitter past laid bare on the pages, a sweet overdue forgiveness stimulated and settled. This forgiveness was granted towards others, towards myself.

With a solemn soul I share them with you, the hurt and the healing. May they be soothing words to your wounds. I remember that my words may be another's healing. But these aren't my words, though spilled from my pen–rather a record of events. This encourages me to fuel forwards, trudging through the tough times to unlock a strength with common understanding.

nightfall

habits

—

Little leech, inches itself
steadily upon my elbow,
slipping slowly onto my forearm.

Staying awhile,
almost unnoticed,
a few more accompany,
incremental weights.

Simultaneously,
they burrow their teeth deep,
sinking into my skin.

But I extract,
enduring their painful fangs,
until they are starved, shriveled,
almost absent.

isolation's induction

—

It all started with isolation.

Cardboard boxes unpacked,
leaning against the cold, white wall.

A room meant to hold old Christmas trees,
sleeping bags and boxes.

A single string leading up to a sole lightbulb,
I tugged the rope to illuminate my new living space.

I should have seen it then,
the demons hiding within each crevasse,
engrained in the wooden planks and dusty drywall,
lurking beneath the unfinished space between wall and
floor.

I managed to fit in a travel-sized foldable bed,
stiffly suppressed within the corner,
limiting the unoccupied floor to a solitary carpet square–
small enough to be filled by a cross-legged posture,
large enough to hold a mess of prowling terrors.

I would sleep during the day,
and wake with a broken dial,
night or noon,
this windowless room.

Thoughts of darkness were thrown during twilight,
ricocheting off the walls and boomeranging back.

Water bottles became brimming with liquor,
makeup bags concealed cocaine,
amidst the pitch-black room were prescription pills,
marked with a non-matching name.

Every morning I'd leave,
and circle back within the afternoon,
trapped in a cocoon I created,
laden with isolation,
a repeated rhythm,
fueling the fire.

This was the room,
where the walls were carved like my skin,
where I wrote countless suicide notes,
and where I learned that I had to get out.

shatter the glass
—

Insecurity is
not a genetic trait,
rather taught.

When you stare at yourself
for a stretched second,
the reflection is lost,
only shapes remain,
and fraudulent thoughts
are formed.

They fester, and spoil–
putting up a flawed facade.

porcelain doll

—

Crippled,
crouching over a bowl,
with twice-chewed lunch,
spit back onto a platter.

Powdering up my face,
wiping the corners of my lips–
pop in a throat lozenge,
for the smell,
for the sting.

high school

—

A martyr for no cause.

depression

—

When a drizzle is so faint,

you almost can't see it,
you almost can't feel it–

until you become damp.

before school

—

Parked within the cul-de-sac,
a few blocks past my house,
preparing to smoke an early
cigarette before school.

Even though the breeze was biting,
and my windows were lined with frost,
I rolled them completely agape,
matching my open-mouth morning yawn,
where cigarette smoke escaped.

I deceptively deduced–
if I dwelled within the morning,
they'd desert by daybreak.

They still lingered, though.

Thoughts that
I'm not good enough
swirl around, and embed
within my seat's upholstery,
intermingling with ideas,
hanging in my hair.

Drawing in a deep breath of toxicity,
I stay with it, meditating;
they are the cigarettes stored
within the glove compartment,
shuffled between coffee-stained,
moth-eaten papers with printed letters.

The ash would scatter across my dashboard,
and sprinkle throughout all aspects
of the accurate reality,
unconsciously fueling my anxiety–
allowing it to seep into every detail,
engrained in every essential.

And the idea that I deserved to be in pain,
would cause me to reach for another,
polluting my lungs, sullying my thoughts.

i never slept anyway
—

Sitting at a dining room table,
staring at the wood grooves and grains.

Subtle curiosity,
deviates into conversation.

An empty cylinder,
the color of marigolds,
rolls across the maple table
that matched the color of my eyes,
the words came quick–

I couldn't sleep.

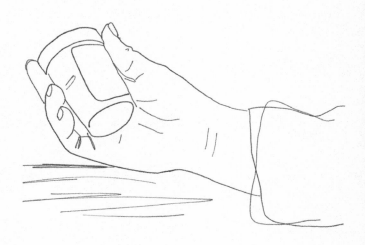

domino

—

White blocks
with inky dots,
soiled, stacked–
slip, fall, tumble.

distracted
—

Closed off,
the light gets choked.
For there are no windows,
to let in the luminance.

Withdraw,
the gold turns to grey,
the great becomes granular–
leaving only weighty
rocks to remain.

Exhausted,
when eyes become heavy–
and dew drops roll–
slowly shutting,
missing the radiance
the wet floor reflects.

at least once a day
—

Hypersensitive
with every mirror,
I stand in front of myself,
staring eye-to-eye,
mind racing rapidly—
its prominence paralyzes
my physical being.

Slumped over, sunken eyes,
lips slightly open.

Seeing this face,
it isn't my own—
cheekbones pronounced,
they lost their color—
which echoes the
void in my voice.

Eyes embody the
outline of my pupil;
they don't smile anymore.

Hair on the floor,
and collecting
between my fingers—
short, brittle nails,
bitten to mask their cracks.

Tiny arms, too wide,
I don't remember a realistic size.

Wondering how the wood
would frame my face,
or what color velvet,
would match this
pale skin, hollow mind.

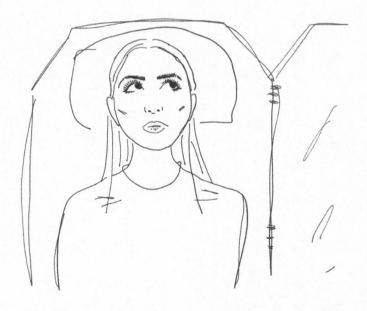

scattered pieces
—

How long does it take
to be at breaking point,
before you're broken?

deceit

—

Recited relentlessly,
cycled by cognition,
stretched onto a banner
within my bedroom,
slung by a thin thread
punctured through paper.

It read, just let go–
an ode to my numbness,
a constant reminder,
to create a chasm, a canyon,
encouraging self-apathy.

the after-party

—

Wanting to go into oncoming traffic,
getting splinters in my fingers
from breaking into houses.

vile vice
—

Cherry drops spill.

Prior, a pause for delusional gain,
now haunts into sleepless nights.

Seeping into the floor,
smudging, staining,
sheets soaking from salty tears
and striking scarlet.

Lukewarm on the outside,
but otherwise frozen.

Pulling and snapping and
etching by the second.

too-thin teeth

—

A deep deception,
a prison of the mind and body.

Careless words thrown at me,
worth worn down to bones,
transferring torment
to the skin that wrapped them.

I held the hand of deception,
coping through control.

Counting each spoonful,
shifted to counting each piece.

But you can only dice
a strawberry so many ways,
tiny slices rationed out for the day.

An overwhelming weight of hatred
swelled within my stomach,
once it rumbled is when it bruised,
black and blue.

Eyes sinking
deeper
and
deeper,
as workout regiments
began before the stars
scurried away.

My actions drove my body
to physical disfunction,
delusion disdained
vital signs.

Opacity of my teeth,
as transparent as my disease.
Eyes-watered, ribs exposed.
The shame burned
as bad as the acid reflux.

Best friend betrayal.

predators

—

Encircled by vicious predators,
sitting within a cold garage,
criss-crossing my legs with arms folded.

Empty beer cans were scattered,
shuffled towards the outer edges.

I was invited over as prey;
the atmosphere had spiders
crawling upon my body,
nesting within my stomach.

The predators were encroaching, circling–
the room swelled; they were preparing
their pounce.

Hollow compliments were
thrown into my direction,
closing in closer,
and disapproval swept
their faces when discarded,
though they persisted.

I saw through the act they were
trying to press, for they were transparent;
alcohol diluting their bloodstream.

They were getting nearer,
the three men that intended
to feast on my ignorance.

Pressure was placed on my presence,
matching my crocodile nightmares–
though instead of achieving consciousness,
I wanted to plunge into a deep sleep,
escaping the snare they were carefully placing.

I was allocated a bedroom,
a mattress in the corner with a single sheet.

I quickly hurried and
latched the door, locked it
and twisted the knob–
fastened in place.

I found a sliver of ease and safety,
within this unknown room,
dirty laundry met the
outdated wood-paneled walls,

I had escaped.

I rested my head and my eyes flickered,
as I dozed off to solitude for the night.

That was when I awoke.
Daylight had not yet dawned
and the room was still dark.

I felt another body
within the locked room.

I was not alone.

I had played into their snare,
for they had switched their approach.

My pants had been undone
by hands that weren't my own,
and another was working to satisfy
their own sick pleasure.

I felt frozen, helpless.

Denounced and disgusted,
I ran out of the room,
past the damaged doorknob.

I ran towards the only familiar face,
within this unfamiliar home,
and spent the rest of the blackness in a car.

Antagonistic vulnerability, sleepless,
sub-zero temperatures.

That night I caught a cold.

broken and bleak
—

When time pauses within the worst moments.

self speculating

—

How can you curse a God that you don't believe in?

insane

—

An outside labeled identity,
carved so dreadfully deep, it became me.

My existence is insane,
heavily littered with hallucinations
and intoxication–an unforgettable,
immutable rattle and racket.

Sober thoughts,
a mixed-up jumble of chaotic chatter–
quick erosion to my conscience,
eating itself to apathy.

A lifeless shell,
with an endless cycle,
insane, insane.

Those words stuck like color to paint,
and dripped like paint, too;
a relentless echo,
with raging repercussions.

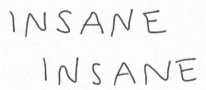

suddenly

—

I see it replay.
A cinematic horror.
I wonder when the memory will fade,
for it is as vividly paralyzing,
as that night itself.

Constrained to my subconscious,
itching for an escape.

day to nightmares

—

Plunging into a restless slumber,
disoriented and frightened.

Night terrors
were a habitual pattern,
waking within a blank,
raven room.

Drops from dream's despair,
left a sopping pillow,
with makeup smeared
and stinging my face.

My dear brother would shake me
awake, in attempts to alleviate me from
my audible screams–they'd leave me
pulling and prying my skin; a pinch
wasn't enough to assume consciousness.

He thought I was being attacked
within my room– and I was, too,
when my eyes were pressed shut.

For my nighttime felt so real,
subconscious collecting faster than
you think; daytime monsters seizing
sleep.

I helplessly reached for a bottle of
tiny pills–zolpidem tablets,

initially on occasion,
now a nocturnal routine.

They started bleeding into my daytime
hours, crushed and ingested when I was
away from my bed.

It was hard for me to decipher dreams
from day, unconsciously present, forgetful
and in another reality; pain was prevalent,
and relief's likelihood–a hallucination.

In a continual state of escaping the other,
reality was meddled into a non-stop nightmare.

high and hangover

—

Enveloped within an endless eclipse, I've felt bound and burdened for as long as I can remember. I forget the sensibility of sunshine–a distant resemblance–that may have solely been a self-contrived mirage that was never truly experienced.

I stumble out to the sidewalk. It has our house number spray-painted on the side of the cold, cracked concrete with a white background highlighting the charcoal numbers. This is where I sit and smoke at one in the morning, while the rest of my family sleeps soundly within their beds. This is where the thoughts come–mangling each molecule, binding me bit by bit.

There is a domino effect of desperation, a sequence of the surreal. My life has been encased in this dingy darkness, anxious to find a lucent light. But within the blackness of bedtime, the only nocturnal glimmer that remains invariable are the stars within the sky, and the several moons. My isolated alleviation lies within a sealed transparent bag of white dust. Even the cognitive outburst of its motility evokes saliva to instantly pool beneath my tongue. I get lost in its beautiful and vibrant flash of white and lively purple, sitting alone on this sidewalk square–emphatically hypnotized by its high. This is my only source of happiness, an ecstasy I cling to, an incredible florescent glow. This light is what I long for; I'm captivated by cocaine's euphoria.

This is the lightning.

The single flash, its vein-like electricity. Once it strikes, it immediately dissipates. A dense fog drowning out even the stars, and depression ambushes each atom–breaking me apart with detachment. I am within the dead of night, secluded from even myself, flooded with anxiety, waves of hatred, harm and hurt. I want my hands to rip out of the skin I've been bound to, escaping into the center of the earth–and with a crave that compels to my core–I want to see the lightning again.

Building canyons between lines, anticipating for lightning to strike. After ingesting each freckle of the chalky grain, the foul taste settles within the back of my throat as my bloodstream becomes a brewing storm. The electric burst overtakes me, a delusive delight, and ends so quickly.

I want to see the lightning again. For the fog is a thick loiter now, and stays cloudy for days. The moons have been diluted within the default day, and stars were another self-created illusion.

The only light I witness is permitted through the lightning strikes, the bright white lines. A fixation making even the bolt marred, not as bright as it once was. I've been pulled deeper and deeper into the opaque thunders. The lightning sets ablaze, mercilessly burning everything, ash remaining in the jet stream.

The depression crawls within. It acts as though it is my body–with only the light being a destructive, fiery force: fogging all light, fogging all faith, fogging all hope.

It's the high and the hangover.

addiction
—

It is the grasp of two hands,
wrapped around my neck.

Loosening when partaking,
then immediately constricting,

tighter than before.

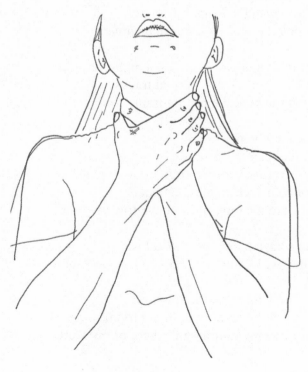

claustrophobia

—

Too close, too close.

If others get too close,
they may peer into the unfiltered, the raw—
seeing the chaos that's secreted behind my smile,
my body abiding to the insanity which inhabits.

My stomach swells,
at the thought of them getting too close.

For they may find that empty plates and
bathroom stalls are dear friends,
and that the scale is a sworn enemy.

That midnight workouts are a nightly routine—
that I'd tug near the railroad tracks,
running next to the rolling train.

They may be my family,
and decipher my distance—
an effort to save them from my reality,
I isolate myself to eliminate pain.
(They are the only ones I have true love for.)

I can't have them come too close,
or they will know how broken I've become.

They may find that the scissors,
knives, and needles within my room
aren't just for trimming the hem of my skirt,

or that the tampon applicator didn't dissemble
itself within my purse,
that the mascara smeared on the wall
was once arranged into words,
written to myself:

Ugly, fat, alone, forgotten, insane.

They may find out that I
self-medicate my depression,
with anecdotes that offer temporary relief–
though imposing side effects
that perfectly escalate prior symptoms.

I get claustrophobic at the speculation
of someone venturing too close–
for I've convinced myself,
that the minute they know I've melted,
from the mess in my mind,
is the moment they'll scatter–
spilled salt.

Distancing even myself from the
vision I'm seeing, the reality I'm facing,
I often conspire ways to further from myself,
to vacate these bending bones.

For even I have gotten,
too close, too close.

the cliff
—

The moon was shaped
like a fingernail clipping,
and hung in the sky,
stale and stagnant.

For night's shadow,
the utter absence,
dulled dimmer than most.

I laid crumbled on the asphalt,
within the bike lane of a deserted street.

Heartbroken and alone,
I stared at the sky with
tears stinging my pores.

In a rage, I snatched the keys to my car,
and drove towards the mountains
that laid stubbornly within the distance.

Face emotionless,
mind blank,
I was driving towards my demise,
listening to the voice of ruin.

As I stepped out of my car that night,
the cold brought shivers to my spine.
The wind brought me towards
the edge of a boulder,
with a steep and rocky drop.

The fall would paralyze or break a limb,
but would leave a rocky pulse,
rather than a flatlined plateau.

This is when I reached for the keys,
in search of greater depth
or an alternate fall,
one which would ensure
to end my heavy head.

That's when the grace of God cut my car off,
the unnoticed little throttle sunk down to show empty.

Frustrated and aggravated,
I dialed the only phone number that I could confide,
and my brother came rolling up the dusty drive.

Flustered at why
I was within the mountains
at five in the morning,
we both shivered and sat in silence
as his tires treaded against gravel;
his silence meant he understood.

I was struck with defeat in every area,
my mind was sopping with darkness–
I thought that this was my last night of life,
but I was saved,

and rebirth was rooting in my veins.

reincarnation

—

An atmosphere inhaled,
immersing toxicity
and battered mindsets–
absconding to such depths,
I almost drown.

Leaving the well-acquainted,
welcomed temptations,
the vices ingrained
into my everyday.

For bones are breaking,
bearing the weight
of malnourishment,
addiction to the void.

With cocaine cravings–
a strong self-gratifying structure,
in need of a richter scale shake.

A hollow mind mixed up,
in vacating all I know—
in hopes of exchanging breath
with the wide open air,
where the black-eyed Susan
blooms from broken.

nightfall

—

My frigid fingers–
each acting as an antique door's hinge–
fumble to grasp this pen.

It is nightfall.
Within these hours, we dwell–
upon the significant, the weighty.
During dusk, we venture,
wandering within thoughts
which swell and broaden.

But when winter emerges,
the night consumes the afternoon–
the somber weeping into the daytime.

For our reflection is brought to our attention,
as the sun settles and we amble into nightfall.

An entire season of dedication,
devoted to holding the mirror to our mind.
And as the year comes to close,
an explosion of sparkle and gold appears
as an array of blinding hope.

New beginnings enlightened,
we are inspired by the frenzy of fireworks–
a fresh introduction.
But we are never concluded,
even if the ending digits are altered.
Our determination isn't deduced

to the rise of a new year.

Yet everyday is energized with celebration.
As we ascend, our aspirations awake with us.

The golden glow each daybreak,
a brisk awakening.

To shed the premature state–
a cocoon of our past perception,
liberating the dreams of self-renewal.

This endless opportunity,
staggers at the edge of your actions,
arising even within the depth of midnight.

morning air, morning light

lavender

statued
—

We've created ourselves,
into a beautifully marbled statue.

Lined with diamonds
that steal a sparkle from the sky,
laden with red rubies.

At one time our existence was bare,
allowing the cool wind
to whisk around our face,
beneath our chin,
earth piecing beneath our feet–
pure.

But through the acclimation of desensitization,
all diminished to our confining cages,
closer than skin,
self-constructed.

Decorated with chains,
looking-glass ornaments,
captivated.
The illusion of
many gold lined layers.

This instant delight and allure,
eventually callouses, growing cold–
jaded by the gems that burden our bodies.

This extension we've composed,

veil of entrapment,
destined to our death.

We remember how
we would move with the wind,
a memory mesmerizing–
yet notice, now we hardly waver.

With a weighted mind,
we muster up the idea,
the freedom gained,
if granted the gentle
currents of the air.

Ruins of several similar statues lay–
beings which had happened to escape
their confining creation.

We marvel though strained by heaps of marble,
believing our stone's density a greater distress.

We coax ourselves,
abandoning notions of aspiration.
For if the shell would somehow deteriorate,
our feet would fumble.

The uncertainties of the future
stir up complacency.
This encasing has become our security
which distances us–
our identity is in the etchings of the stone,
the podium we have been built on.

And one day,
as our eyes are heavy and encrusted,
we see the horizon.

For our etchings will erode over
and the diamonds will become dirty;
but our freedom is the uncertain beauty
we cannot afford to live without,
but could never tangibly afford.

This is when we tap upon the shell,
and our stone shatters out like glass.

In awe of the gumption we have mustered up,
we quickly feel regret
and try to piece together the image
we have nurtured for so long.

But then the wind sweeps through.

At a halt,
we hold the rubble of our
past selves in our hands;
our eyes lift back to the horizon.

We are

free

and

complete.

Movement has never been so liberating.

We are exposed and raw;
we throw the pieces of the past,
the falsely fastened selves.

Sinking our feet into the cold earth once again,
we run whichever way the wind guides us.

genesis

—

Pursuing a stray thought,
bending prospective ambition,
into a self-invitation
of a great-distance migration,
at month's notice.

Eager to unload the burdens,
displacement assembled.

My empty, sour stomach settled,
when I received my mother's embrace,
as I packed my bones and belongings
into the dusty blue Oldsmobile,
that shared an age with me.

Arriving on Christmas,
my fresh start, my new beginning,
wrapped itself in a bow of blue skies
and snowy grounds.

My possessions were few,
they were starting from scratch, too.

Only a pillow, comforter,
and space heater–gifted by my sister,
inhabited my new bedroom.

Where time stands still,
carefully considering every intake,
observing habitual inclination.

It was a radical debut,
escaping the sharp teeth of addiction,
that lurked in the shadows of surrounding,
now in the place of rehabilitation.

A few bad habits lingered,
pruned away,
and as my empathy grew,
I became apathetic towards
the dissipating detachment.

I was no longer
fastened to the flaws–instead,
the opportunity of redemption renewed.

i n t r o d u c t i o n

—

The notebook was blank, suggesting to be filled with sketches, with several pages meeting this demanding expectation.

The illustrations were almost effortless, and birthed by my brother's hand–detailed, perfectly shaded and blended. My brother always exceeded in any facet of art that caught his attention, a trait I relentlessly pursued to reflect, but consistently fell short.

I shuffled around in my bag, fishing for a writing instrument; the pen I found was stolen from a waitress at a Chinese restaurant. Though spotty between strokes, I decided to etch a few notes and scratches, to let my pen wander without any real aim.

After scribbling out a few indistinguishable drawing attempts, I began to feverishly write a letter.

The blank page then became filled with ink, addressed to my mother. This letter contained a shuffled synopsis of my new endeavors since moving a thousand-and-some miles distant.

I was enamored with the potential of the future, but still blinded by a broken glass lens. But with each tiny word inscribed, came restoration. This was the first time I could visually comprehend my current state, dissolving each detail to paper.

I snatched out the letter from the metal bindings and
spoke the words written to my sister, sharing the unfetter
my mind felt when I wrote. With such encouragement,
she coupled words with scripture, tying it to truth. This
inspired my pen to propel, extracting each piece of past.

This was my introduction to healing.
This was the introduction to my unfolding.

settling in

—

Enduring until end day,
burning till the ash
reaches my bite.

Looking through the lunette,
echoing my face–
rebounding.

Webbed together by veins,
feeling vital fluid flow–
circulating.

I've always tried
to determine my death,
but have never endeavored
to take hold of today.

ohio

—

The temporary state,
where the dream of renewal,
is tangible.

pieces
—

For actions were
always deliberate,
born from unconscious
pre-meditation.

Every reflection
is pregnant with action–
entertained,
encouraged,
accepted,
sinking from our mind,
polluting our marrow.

There may be no eyes drawn,
though ours bloodshot open–
seeing,
noticing,
knowing.

Without the relief of a blink,
we stare into the glass walls of intent;
bearing the weight and burdens,
inescapably aware.

Each aspect within ourselves,
painfully addressed.

Our humble attack,
is beautifully sobering.

alignment
—

Just because we've become
accustomed to our own sour,
doesn't make it sweet.

vices
—

How can a hollow hole
be filled with things
of no substance?

getting out
—

Diverging,
traveling out past
the movements
of my single sense,
for it shifts and falls.

It falls short.

I'm vacating outside
these ever-wavering
tides of reflex,
venturing apart from
this snow–globe mind–
where all I'm aiming
to obtain are still flakes,
always shaken up again.

I'm excelling out;
embarking through
the momentous mountains
and ocean outlook,
living within the sun-skied view.

Soaring through,
outstretched yet vastly held.

salvation

—

Darkness was so thick–
seeping beneath the door,
snagged throughout my hair,
stinging my skin,
soaking into every pore–
sharp stabs in my narrow mind.

But in the garage,
thick with cigarette smoke,
lived late night revival.

He is the structure of strength,
muscle and veins,
the bones constructing my frame.

I will never tear apart,
rather thrive–
living in unison,
living in light.

Permanent presence,
from renouncement to rebirth.

absolution

—

Existing to remember,
existing to forget.

Lingered lapses let go–
so instead of holding on,
presumed unspoken dismissal.

Liberated through
speech and heart,
paralleled.

The intertwined has been untangled,
with hope and healing held.

freedom
—

A feeling that seems
so familiar, a coming home,
though this territory is a foreign field.

No longer does the weight
shift heavy between my shoulders,
for I have a new anatomy,
created with divine composition.

The sky is a shade more saturated,
a song sung with each encounter.

Dust glitters, in the sky, for you.
Grand entrance into every room.

An anew awareness,
awakened and alive.

vista

—

You can't see this
kaleidoscope of color
if viewed in the dark.

bliss

—

Wholly and completely held,
loving without limitation,
the vivacious veracity–bliss.

lungs

—

It's known that
when we breathe,
it's shallow—
storing stagnant air.

Until we draw
deep, deep down
into the depths
of our lungs.

tracking

—

Picking up breadcrumbs,
piecing together
the origin thought,
I lost hours ago.

hidden

—

A poisonous ivy seed planted,
sprouted by your thoughts,
it intertwines your mind.

Silently suppressing
the ivy inward–
trimming the stems–
careful not to uncover.

Cautious, its curls are concealed,
it twists around your lungs
and extends within your stomach,
packed from skin-to-skin,
the seedling's permission
has grown a greenhouse.
Stretching, entangling,
consuming, constricting.

Shearing to eradicate
only plucks leaves off the vine.
Sowed deep, subduing all efforts–
propagating, producing.

An overwhelming strive,
a point of desperation
summons courage,
adrenaline strength
tugs at the root,
excavating from the inside.

Purging to light,
the stalk suffocates,
vine bridles,
releasing the hold;
an unbinding dilatation–
inward emancipation.

cardiac arrest

—

If the audio-identification sends shudders,
then the heart uncovers a chronic convulse.

breathing   spell

—

I catch my visual echo.

My eyes slowly scan
a tired, yet trying, face.

The in-between.

Midnight hair,
daylight skin.

A balance,
tipping at the weight
of emotion.

But feelings are fleeting, and
right now does not last forever.

I can force the proportion
to lean into progression–
if I keep trying,
identifying and extracting,
an endless pursuit.

A pinch of peach,
returning to my cheeks.

I bridge between
this duplicate of my being–
as foreign as an old photo.

Resemblances begin to arise.

I remember these eyes,
lining of my face,
fuller hair.

I am slowly slipping into my skin,
rather than an onlooker's
third-party perspective.

I rub my hands together,
hearing the gentle friction
of palm-between-palm.

My skin, my body,
a temple.

recovery
—

I was fooled to believe
that recovery is only
an implausible dream,
a mirage in the distance.

But as I become acquainted
with the heaping work,
though highly daunting,

the recollection of recognition,
refreshes with fruition;
I fasten myself to the fixed unfamiliar.

I esteem each affirmative action,
now a methodical melody,
becoming a harmonic habitual.

hard times
—

Even the embers expose their most
constricting corners.

Unlocking buds that could only bloom,
from that hurt that burnt inside of you.

the choice is mine

—

I'm capable of nullifying the numb,
deeply rooting my frame of mind in the infallible–
rather than the temporary temperament.

For even the redwoods defy gravity,
stretching towards the skyward's solace.

identity

—

Identity is not something
that can be cut, dyed or colored.

It isn't tangible,
nothing that can be
weighed or starved.

It is something that is found,
the intention for creation.

Not image nor talent,
not family or friends–
but a formerly fixed affinity,
affirmed by the cameo of Christ.

unity with myself

—

A marriage of
transformation–
for better or worse.

Committed to continue committing,
carrying out my oath to elevate,
pursuing passionate progression.

Striving to serve maturation,
'til death do us part.

hand in hand

—

Amends–
mending.

Mind's–
mending.

p a s t i m e

—

When I began my
favorite pastime–
my nose would bleed,
and I wasn't strong enough
to read Edgar Allen Poe–
but these were the words
my therapist spoke.

My pen became well-acquainted
within my hand, dancing together
within the day, and somberly sketched
beneath the slight shivers of our
family's grown aspen at twilight.

It grew with me,
travelled cross country–
tracking rehabilitation,
sparking an intense love
between introspection and letters.

Blossoming and enveloping me,
not the origin of healing, rather resource–
a gift embedded into my fibers.

For writing is the pastime
in which I stop time,
allowing hours
dedicated towards–
exhalation, feeling,
thinking, growing.

reservoir of euphoria
—

Thoughts are ever-flowing,
multiplying based off of
the self-admission given.

For we can stimulate
a spark in sentiment,
improving our state of mind.

This is the reservoir of euphoria,
decorated with the magnificence
of the magnolia trees,
foliage climbing free,
mingling with the peony's promise of hope.

Some thoughts sneak into our minds,
holding endeavors to deplete and drain–
to wither the florets within the trees,
the strangle scorch of desert's demise.

With weeds to choke out the peonies–
leaving the land desolate and dusty,
while building a dam,
constricting the river's
running ripple into the reservoir.

Thoughts are ever-flowing,
multiplying based off of
the self-admission given.

Let's tear out all the weeds,

breaking down the dam
with precision.

Rock-by-rock,
the removal of the dam
is more tedious than its making.

Trickled through.

Water is able to reach
its becoming habitat.

The trickle becomes a flow,
and with diligence,
the water is able to crash through.

Restoring the vast landscape,
promoting the thoughts which inspire;
the well-being of the mind.

Euphoric splendor elevating throughout,
percolating outside even our environment.

For thoughts are ever-flowing,
multiplying based off of
the self-admission given.

why i write

—

The more leaked letters
printed to paper–
the less words watering
the whirlpool within my head.

how i was

—

Fumbling alongside the hills–
heavily coated in thick green grass–

trudging along, seeing what is
seemingly our destiny,

though only following
the backs of our eyelids.

measuring progress
—

The fuzzy faint shapes
when eyes are closed tight–
seemingly there, yet not evident,
disappearing if you look too long.

Measured on an elusive scale,
converting past perception to current state,
balancing the old tendencies
with circulating habits.

It's witnessing heat rise
from the asphalt in the distance,
a mirage of memory in the standing's scene.

amidst all

—

Wind tosses naked branches,
scratching the side of the window
and its sill, a restless rustling.

Yet peace still envelops,
steadfast and sure,
my heart is calm and quiet.

night to daydreams
—

Uninterrupted slumber,
dancing stars within the sky.

No longer am I robbed,
of this dewy-eyed bliss,
a cascade of comfort–
knives and scissors exchanged for
shapes and vibrant colors.

Surrounded by safety,
arising with energy.

For the ante meridiem
flicker of the eyelash,
retains a rush of excitement
from the night's cinema.

The sinkholes
that lined my eyes dissipate;
iris, full of life–
for even deep sea creatures,
deep dream monsters,

dissolve once dragged to light.

relapse
—

I dropped my pen,
for almost a year,
due to self-doubt.

That's when they came.

The crescendoing
cumulonimbus,
collecting clutter,
casting overcast inclinations–
disorganized,
a recurring conveyer belt,
piling against a wall.

Relapsed–
with my eating,
thought-seeking,
my writing,
empty hands.

But I wouldn't let them stay.

I shuffled the wind,
conversed in quiet prayer,
and loud praise–
my mind disputed the deceit,
and the pen laid back in my hand.

realignment

—

A jolt in calibration,
mental askew,
but alignment found,
in the alive.

autumn reflection

—

Crisp air.

Drips are steadily streaming
from my eyes, and seep out
my chapped nose.

You saw into me–
your mind filled with mine,
a clear vision, though frosted–
the deception in my perception.

My despair, the thick scent of tree sap,
fragile condition–dry and departing,
the subtle decay of leaves
breaking within the draft,
and swirling in the air.

I ventured with no vision,
anticipating my stumble and downfall.

You disentangled
my mangled meditation.

Eyes have been thawed,
now piercing up towards the skies.

patterns
—

A relentless domino effect,
diligent intent in each piece,

careful and steady,
not letting our minds slip for a second.

e q u a l

—

Outright action
all the same.

Debt only increases,
if our antipathy of one,
eclipses another.

For the outright action
is all the same.

fullness

—

Healing is heavy,
brewed from hot water.

Dewy and dense
lavender twigs,
dilution from diffusion,
percolating.

Cup's depth,
strong and sweet,
forgiveness to freedom.

running lines
—

Never parallel,
rather intersecting,
moving onward.

Progressing forward with healing,
and forever forgiven.

time

—

If a revelation can happen
within a single moment,
advancement abounding
in this tiny timeframe,
to think of all the–

minutes,
hours,
days,
months,
years–

a daunting happening,
yet dazzling insight,
arises.

moment
—

I'm meant for this moment;
shaded by a dense stratus cloud,
among the purple and white blooms,
with leaflets lining the sticks in the sky.

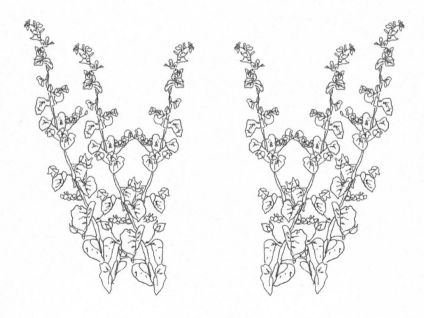

raw

—

Once I understood:

my wrong is not worse than yours,
your wrong is not worse than mine

is when I identified forgiveness for you,
forgiveness for myself.

truth
—

For forgiveness feels stagnant–
almost regression,
but plunges us towards the pivot of light–
an all consuming acceleration.

introspection
—

Each minute, refining.
I may be within the patient,
but I am not amidst a pause.

golden gaze

breathing

—

Sipping in a slow, billowing breath;
lungs savoring every bit of oxygen,
inflating my lungs.

My inhale is a strong wind
which catches each fragment of thought–
the fragrance of the early morning,
intertwines with the soil's saturated aroma,
laced with the wild marigolds.

They hang thick
within the air,
a gale swirling,
and with a pause–
allows all to float
and settle in my sternum,
a scene set solely
for the chickadee's chatter.

The deep exhale,
completely clearing,
wholly ventilating,
exuding all.

This is clutter
that does not correlate,
I notice how each piece
of lingering thought
is expelled.

Soothed and still,
encompassing balance
mind and body relaxed.

here

—

Embracing the present,
mind's rearrange–
from constricting
and manipulating,
to open palms,
and a mouthful of praise.

poise
—

There are periods within our lives where patience is forced upon us. I find myself frequently residing in these hazy mornings of hiatus. These moments tend to stimulate an array of emotion and introspective thought.

The wind cannot be coerced on a calm day, nor can hot water be boiled solely from desire. Often, I find that even the nimbostratus billows are transparent, unable to drown out the rays of the sun. I become sober to the familiar posture of this state, and I'm able to recognize that these lapses within living are intentional. They are premeditated, fixed, and will remain so until reoriented.

This revelation of staying within the quiet resonates; it steeps like lavender tea—strong yet gradual, saturating my thoughts. I revisit realignment, a well-familiar friend, one I intend to visit far more often than I do. In these times, I invite it to dwell—to watch the sun rise and sip my tea with me—proportioning my precedences.

Recollecting what's internal, priorities and their significance becomes magnified. I notice that when I'm within an overwhelmingly occupied occasion, this act tends to slip away, overlooked.

I recall each savored rumination, and their natural practices. I reevaluate their manifestation and its magnitude. By continuously interpreting and soaking within this stillness, I'm able to ensue growth.

This aurora exposes matter, cultivating reclamation. This patience has encouraged peace, devoting time towards identifying thorns and its process of plucking them from my flesh. Focused forgiveness of myself, and others–truly understanding the progression of relief.

The future will be rapid but since I have realigned myself, I know that no compromises will be taken. Even during the dawn, as this current outlook overturns towards the next, this sequence has transitioned me gracefully towards the sunrise.

This expands my anticipation. For I am rejoicing towards the future, even if I am waiting within today. This is the foggy dew with its humble humidity. By choosing to become saturated with stillness' stature, this serenity has become a nectarous honey, balanced with the tranquility and calmness of chamomile.

hope

—

It's when my eyes are shut,
but the golden light leaks through.

intention

—

Life is always honey
but sometimes we just choose
to see the stinger.

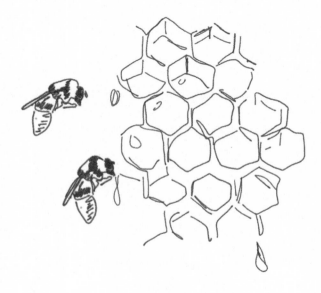

high noon
—

Knowing the sun
will inevitably rise to its peak,
but patiently waiting for this moment.

Let's ease into calm expectation,
healing and mending–
existing within this existing time.

it spills
—

Cuts,
scars,
scratches,
connected with
a changed connotation.

Blood no longer broods,
its bond, embodies reformation.

We have been
mended by cuts and scars,
a somberly beautiful gift–
no longer exchanged with anxiety.

Obedience and diligence,
dilutes all darkness.

every morning
—

After night, it's blissful light.

peace
—

The candle's flame flickers,
walls flashing it's gentle hue,
with wax pooling slowly, settling.

When silence is truly such,
meeting the promise of its name.

Mind calm, soul soothed.

water-streaked window
—

I use to be claustrophobic
within my own skin, my thoughts
took up too much room,
memories slipping into
remembrance
in various forms;
flashes of distress–
triggered by words,
subconscious realizations linked
to slumbered images of my youth–
each moment crowded with hallucination.

But I gave these thoughts names,
either escorting them out,
or inviting to stay.

They are given careful thought,
though thoughts themselves.

No longer a whirlpool of raging rivers–
not a storm from the sky,
nor a mental monsoon–
rather a basin of opportunity,
with patient reflection.

Amidst an ongoing intermission,
to digest and decompose this introspection.

I identify the derivatives,
and nurture the words written.

They develop restoration,
laced with conviction,
releasing a stimulating serenity.

c o n v i c t i o n

—

When the mundane becomes recognized,
the otherwise unnoticed
shifts to a splinter in your side.

A bitter annoyance,
background agitation.

Embedded, then pried out.
Foreground irritation, initial sting,
yet a bittersweet that flows to honey.

A highlight, to pinpoint–
other splinters, fractures, needles.

Admonish the issue,
pushing through to breakthrough.

what i've found to be true

—

Our deliverance comes from God,
but the obedience comes from us.

transmitted, channeled

—

That aureate light,
a vision from the sun casting
through millions and millions of miles,
to touch the tops of my toes.

reappearance

—

A small comment that a stranger spoke, sent me
ricocheting to the remembrance of that day.

–

The atmosphere was ambling with air fragranced by
coffee beans, chamomile and peppermint. It was that
open-all-evening coffee shop that always had a blender
on, buzzing in the background. It thrived off chatter, with
the occasional audible chord strung on an acoustic guitar.

I saw him, sitting on a wooden stool in the corner,
scrolling on their community computer. That's when I
was flooded by flashbacks, distracted by the recollection.
This unintended interruption brought my mind to
blank, becoming absent. I stood in front of the barista,
speechless, though I had ordered the same tea for the past
six years at this second-home. I remembered his arms that
grabbed my body against my will.

He rotated his eyes towards the barista counter, each
degree divulging the side-profile that my nightmares were
well accustomed to. I felt the blood rush out of my face,
its pace matched how quickly I fled away from him that
night. For reality had left this memory in the past, but my
trauma remembered it well.

Earthquakes of a heartbeat erupted in my chest and
multiplied into a pounding panic within my temples. My
body was triggering its fight or flight mode.

In that moment, standing beneath the painted ceiling tiles of color, triggers of violation left me feeling trapped. I didn't know what emotion I should have, so I pushed it all out. Should I have punched him in the face, with the brass knuckles that were gifted to me after the incident? Called the police?

I was completely stunned. I felt subdued by the serpent of silence, a slave to anxiety arising. Each footstep stammered, with unsteady hands–I spilled my tea and slipped out the door. I pretended that this was another night terror–I tried to shake myself to forget the reappearance that had happened minutes, hours prior.

–

Years passed before I became fully cognizant of the reappearance. I couldn't even find the words to tell my husband. This moment, writing out these letters, has been one of the few times I confessed that I saw him again. It took me years to tell my husband of the episode–that we walked by strangers, among them, the man who sexually assaulted me.

If I were to run into him again, I'm not certain what my initial reaction would prompt, though I know that healing has softened my heart and calmed my mind. I'd like to think that I'd pull up a stool next to his. I'd tell him that I forgive him fully.

I would tell him that I was able to receive a freedom and love that is overflowing its capacity and is offered to broken people like us. That his identity isn't wrapped or warped by the past mistakes made, that his brokenness is no further cracked or smashed more severely than my own.

This love and forgiveness, freedom by grace is offered to all. I would tell him that the only part of our past that we carry into our future is our testimony.

golden gaze

—

I take a look out towards first light,
and how it pierces through the sky.

This is when my worries dissipate–
for they get lost along the horizon,
trying to reach the sun.

y e l l o w

—

I grab the boots with the marigold stitching interlining the soles and tug them onto my feet by the black-yellow tag. I've devoted today to venture deep within the forest–to savor the company of the trees, the earth and the silence. To savor the time away from familiar surroundings.

I spot two thick sycamore trees a brief distance apart; I tightly fasten my hammock onto their solid trunks with a yellow carabiniere.

Steadying my balance as I lay within, I slouch and look out towards the view. I take in the lake full of blue ripples, lined with dogwood trees–allowing their offering of oxygen to extend to every alveolus. As I look up, I see that the tree's top act as freckles to the sky, with wind strobing the sunlight.

In this glimpse, my mind is clear and still. It acknowledges and environs the bird's call and song, each and every influx. My eyes then are guided to movement within the water, witnessing an orange-yellow snake gliding effortlessly until it reaches the coast. The light is imitated off its slippery scales, echoing the golden glow.

I am completely consumed with a joy that paces through my heart, an unexplainable happiness that crescendos within my being. The darkness of the night is forgotten when staring into the day's beauty, and hardships seem as a vapor in the distance–known, but not abided.

Gratitude never runs out. It is a dandelion–a gossamer dissipating with each inhalation instilled, seeds spreading and swelling within all aspects of my life, budding the cheery flourish. This is the state in which I gravitate towards; a wholeness and completeness within the joy, peace and love that radiates around me.

I carry myself over to the daytime's offered light and plant myself on the dense, velvet pasture as I set my head onto the earth and close my eyes. Gratitude only runs out when I choose not to acknowledge it. But I'm consumed with the soft strokes on the back of my eyelids. It's the incredible warmth which illuminates throughout my core. My thoughts are consumed–communing my mind–spirit stirring as peacefully as the wind within these trees.

morning air,
morning light

c o l o r a d o

—

The air sometimes reminds me of the place where I grew;
the place that left me battered and bruised. The same
land where my eyes would trace the mountains and their
jagged edges. Where even the stubborn boulders would
crumble, giving way beneath my toes, chipping away to a
shatter of spirit.

When I visit back, I am amidst an alternate universe.
My stomach doesn't quite settle–for everything is
familiar, everything is tangible–yet I am not kin to this
surrounding. All of these people are me, but aren't.

The Colorado air ambles among the souls I love; I share
this same breath with them, cycled through the evergreens
and aspens. My lungs hold it for a prolonged period,
rather than hyperventilate from lost hope.

I am sitting, here–at peace, noticing.

I see each rock as it is; I see the ripples in the lake as it
is. My soul has been stirred and shaken since I've left,
tectonic plates emerging convergence. The result is strong.
It is steadfast. It is faithful.

Calamity from the past exchanged for the calm current–an
abounding symphony with freedom stretching out further
than any field of vision. For I aim to venture into fresh
revelation, always climbing a consistent climax, eternally
exponential in elevation.

early today
—

Overtaken by passion,
eyes dancing across the sky,
mesmerized by the majesty woven
into the fibers of the everyday.

For hope harmonizes
and resiliently resounds,
pulsing through my veins,
pounding outside my chest.

This is living,
this is instilling,
this is an ode to restoration.

d i s c e r n m e n t

—

Dew lines my lungs and leaves,
thick enough to withstand summer's glare,
respiration revolves in today's beauty.

The aroma drifts heavily with endless occasion,
possibilities and inspiration—after all,
they were birthed from the morning,
growing to amble within the daytime hours.

As I advance within the day,
the ever-changing,
steadily shifting clouds remind me;
I don't have to be cyclical,
within this pale blue blank canvas.

Instead, I'm wavered,
shifted, altered by the wind—
whether billowing,
or that small, still voice.

Discernment over duties,
risks over routine, bold
like the cumulonimbus brumes.

perspective

—

Acknowledgment of the sun,
how it rises and falls,
yet we are the ones moving.

Other stances placed center-stage–
origins of self-indulgence,
altered to adjust our relativity.

aligned now

—

My mind's posture is poised with extended arms and open palms, addressing an aligned perspective.

For I was amidst the clamored and cluttered, but was not destroyed. Present day dwelling: a scene of quiet basil plants sprouting within a glass jar on the windowsill, a gentle hum of a fan as my husband and little pup are slumbered together within the afternoon shadow. I am filled with gratitude–pen in hand, happiness brimming.

The past, both daunting and detrimental at times, is incredibly important, inaugural to my existence. It's the contrast, a view of the intangible measure of grace that has been poured out.

For light is best seen when contrasted with darkness.

There are still nights where the ominous black descends within my thoughts and loiters a stale stench within my mind. I possess authority; I am able to identify what does not belong, the outlier and eject it out of my thoughts.

That came with practice, too.

When my bare toes meet the cold concrete outside my home, I am reminded that even the moon is a slave to the sun. It resonates its shine, a hope and promise. For even the night has to abide by the light and we will never shift into the darkness.

past our capacity
—

A love,
that saturates all else,
its prevalence paramount.

It embraces–all encompassing,
this love likes to saunter and stay,
it drifts within our bones,
woven into our core–
flowers flourish
from our fingers once found–
and stays top-of-mind.

It sits in our stomach,
soothing peppermint tea,
strong yet sweet.

It is His love,
unique yet vast,
more than the blades in the meadow,
or the grains of sand which line earth's edge,
His love poured into each ocean dew drop.

Unlocked and void of capacity–
yet freely given,
an outrageously astounding outpour.

living

—

Sealing my eyelids together,
lashes intermingling–
light behind my lids dim and brighten,
clouds conversing with the sun,
a delightful dance.

The gentle stroke of the splendor,
sinks into my soul,
thoughts easing–
slowly and lightly
coming into consciousness.

The most beautiful blue,
steady hue, patterned canvas,
serving as the ultimate backdrop
to all below.

cyclical

—

From broken to blooming.

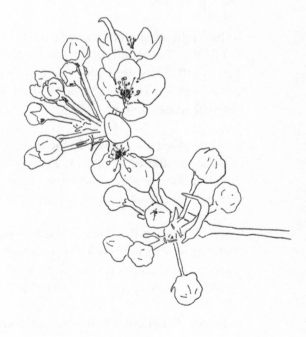

a i r p l a n e

—

Ears popping, my eyes scan the pesticide track patterns
within the circle and square lots below. My eyes meet the
river lines–their origins and their outpour. I watch drops
cluster, together in unison; despite the weightiness of the
world, they create something beautiful for the bystanders
below.

I'm thankful for the view, snapping a few photos every
moment or so, naming the thanks even in the small things:
these papers on my lap, the forty-thousand foot view, the
gentle drops of the aircraft, the chatter of one stranger
helping another.

To the right are a plethora of beautiful billows, foamy
and frothy. To the left, cotton ball clouds lay beneath
the aircraft. They are wind-raked and lightly packed–
translucently texturing the sky. I sip in this space, a
spiritual sense–divine.

We drift along the sunset. In the distance, I study a series
of these smothered sceneries. They remind me of those
shared in view with my husband on our honeymoon
cruise. I don't wish to go back, though.

Eyes are hung in the thick of the fog, unmarred by
nostalgia's notorious spill. Every while further from the
last provokes deeper understanding, prolongated past with
each mile leveling a closer parallel to the sun's stage.

A deeper, richer color saturates our love–kindred to the
day's finale.

b o l d

—

Cyclical life,
the ever-open
ventilation,
empty, dry,
the desert land.

Ever-shifting and flexible,
paint our lives like the clouds–
some days lay and linger,
while others are swift,
scurrying across the globe.

Regardless of circumstance,
they percolate with happiness
and joy; content.

For our scope isn't limited,
rather eternal.

Encompassing these moments,
that define our forever.

Drawing me to drop,
perpending in the pause,
staring into the sky.

Collecting, yet expelling.

I drift within the jet stream,
breaking the cyclical,

deliberately traveling,
towards the direction,
traveling the distance,
of discernment.

atlantic ocean

—

The flashback of the subtle waves'
uninterrupted rhythm,
unrelenting pattern.

Delicate is their design,
without flaw.

Pondering on the attention
invested into each droplet.
Such simplicity refined,
though they've been
around the world.

If such care had been invested
in the artistry of these drops,
in the ripples they create;
in their colors emulating
the epitome of sunrise–
pale to deep,
peach to brilliant resilience,
radiated with no trace of impurities.

I drown in the idea
of how carefully I was created.

flowers

—

We are the peonies,
created beautifully,
always, always, always
growing towards the light.

the memorial tree
—

Smooth skin turns to soil,
as hair intertwines with earth's roots.

Living words
throughout a lifetime–
are living still.

For the dead breathe
through the birch trees,
veined and sewn into the soil.

Intaking, breathing, thriving,
conversing with our lungs–
a vital luxury, miracle, often exploited.

For the nature,
and its intent can impact generations.

clean

—

The mysterious stratus
whisks over the moon,
illuminated, for the stars
still have their ability
to shine through.

It is the crisp,
five in the morning air,
inhaling deep breaths–
ground still wet with rain,
soil moist and easy to churn.

Taking those first strides,
out of the door onto the cold steps–
this is moonlit meditation–
security and strength.

pure

—

Pages empty,
the overflow of characters–
assembled shiftily
through a ball-point pen,
pages filled.

Hearts walking within the park
on afternoon's peak,
with a popsicle leaking
sugary drops on our toes,
feeling light within my spirit.

The opening of the photo album
that collected dust for many years.

The embrace of my mother–
the gentle kiss of my lover.
The countless nights conversing with a brother.

Pure living.

spring
—

Sifting,
flipping through
a half-written journal,
dancing through pages,
between my fingers and palms,
eyes scanning my fumbling pen,
dates depicting two years prior.

I had been departed,
buried, though my bones
were still swaddled with warm flesh–
an accurate array of my former perception:
passionless, half-filled but otherwise empty.

I do spot the seeds, though.

Tiny morsels of text–
surrounding premature revelations,
not yet uncovered, nor integrated.

Funny stanza lines,
detailing death;
I choke on my laughter.

But as I read, I fill to the brim;
writing's a tangible measure,
to unveil the unfolding.

Blossomed past accusations,
and taking notes of trauma–

it was a way to shift,
to move past the negative to neutral.

To thank until I thrived.
I lived within a space of
discontentment and darkness,
until now.

For all I see are golden gifts,
generously wrapped about.

kaleidoscopic love

—

Deep, rich,
vibrant and bright,
ever-wonder, genuinely new,
yet forever-consistent,
in evolving symmetry.

progression

—

How refreshing
is the morning innocence,
crisp elation;
it acts as an internal cleanse,
purifying my perception–
exposing internal progression.

My eyes light up
with the potential of today–
pulsing mind's natural rested state,
amidst the chaotic surroundings,
I can remain calm and content.

The birds sing the chorus of chrysalis,
and the buds soak in the morning dew.

The dawn has
birthed restoration,
all ashes have been
swept away within the night.
I close my eyes and flash a smile.

As the sun awoke to center-sky–
radiating from the horizon,
an awakening also rose in me.

Encouragement embedded,
passion, webbed within my being–
all spun for purpose.

temporary

—

This life may live within our bones–
yet this life is not our own.

belonging

—

A gift planted with purpose–
obedience propagating practice,
persistent perseverance.

The orange tree's florets that flowers fruit,
a blazing azure by background,
vision environed, an uncapped sky.

contradistinction

—

As I stumbled home from work, I rolled out onto my front lawn. Still stiff from winter's shock, I imprinted my elbows, back and bum into the faded yellow grass. Days like these are entirely confounding, to the point where I feel weak within my bones.

These are the days when it seems that former foes are still haunting–trailing every step, plodding. Their facades are frequent: appearing within films I watch, men's deodorant, naïve humor. They are disguised in conversation, or arise through a sudden reaction. These recollections trigger intense emotions, attempting to lure me into a perplexing depth of the mind and body.

It's a hard thing to have a vivid memory–past circumstances stick and stay. I often take intentional interruptions within my day, a second to soak up the present, dismissing any thoughts or anxieties from the past. For when all stars are bursting within my soul, is when the demons attempt to inhabit. It's a hollowing experience. I know that this is not a coincidence– but strategic–for they have witnessed my recovery, perspective switch and current fulfillment.

They aim to plummet my perspective through their whispers in the wind. I refuse. I close my eyes and feel the sun radiate through my skin. I was once overtaken by the depths, smothered and sick but now I push onwards. I persevere within the present. This incredible strength has been acquired only though my Creator.

As I look onto the grey-blue sky, I sip in bottomless breaths. I sit still with a cleansed mind and recount the new ideas that squeeze towards the forefront. A skill learned long ago, a habitual practice from time-to-time needs additional attention–catching a thought before it festers, stopping at a standstill and combatting with scripture. Making a mental inventory, I align my understandings. I am able to recognize the amount of incredible growth experienced within the prior years. My former struggles become more faint and faded with each passing day.

So now, I trade these triggers for triumph. My past to present holds such great contrast–a sweet election of gratitude over guilt, appreciation over all. I stand firm on the truth that is ingrained within me, pushing forwards towards the exponentially flourished future.

grey skies

—

Grey skies still hold a silver lining,
the gentle reminder:
a floodlight is bursting within us.

his promises

—

We must be patient,
flooding with praise–
for this foreshadows
the prolific promise,
a bounty abounding.

Orchards
and their endless fruition–
all favored through faith.

memory

—

In this space,
there are no walls.

Trees budding tiny leaves,
preparation for the
summer's shade supply.

We descend and dwell.

Laying upon blankets
in a field of overgrown grass–
among lilies and onions,
I'm accompanied by my sister,
a soul whose conversation
engulfs greenhouse growth.

The gentle whisper
of the purple hue–a violet,
a creamy, yellow center.

Both penning,
a ponder so silent,
its prominence deafening.

The distance holds the ruckus of insects,
we walk barefoot through grass,
as trees crackle against each other,
wind directing high and low harmonies.

My sister softly reveals–

the deer within short scope–
among them, a doe.

Tentatively,
their distance decreases,
bushy white tail tenses
then tranquil,
as they progress closer
to where we're perched.

This daytime–a dream;
reality's sweet surprise,
shared alongside my sister.

I feel intimate with nature,
inspired by my Maker,
closer to my sister–
and smaller than the tiny,
green spider,
slipping on a stalk,
or the caterpillar
traveling from

violet petal

to

petal.

catching

—

There are moments,
ones that you want to
encapsulate into a bottle,
storing within your
medicine cabinet,
sealed within a jar,
to lather daily.

But these moments,
are the ones that you
have to open your eyes
a little wider,
to catch the full frame.

For these moments,
will pass with time,
but remain with gratitude.

afternoon tug

—

Today's been slipping
by with great ease,
joy spontaneously arranged.

A single, red cardinal,
perches and calls,
beneath the ever-open sky,
on the dogwood branch.

I've entertained the deathly trap–
not good enough–
far too frequent and recent,
than I'd like to admit.

But these past days, weeks,
I've engaged an alter of attitudes,
embracing conviction.

With a wholehearted welcome,
I carefully collect,
in efforts to always obey.

With transparency, I admit–
self-control has been a frail,
forgotten limb, with any weight–
bending, snapping, fatigued.

But each action,
placed in obedience,
offers opportunity.

Robin hops in our grass
to grab a snack;
conviction is a gift.

Sober with sensitivity to even
the seemingly small,
today's perspective is but a light
onto the promised prism of eternity.

Instead of a self-paced progression–
prayer and open-mindedness
will reveal.

I'm called to live a life,
within perennial principals,
always aiming for utmost purity.

But when conviction is muted,
I become lost.

For I can't grow upward
without a solid root,
tackling the area within my life–
uncovered, magnified,
through convictions gentle graze.

contrasting

—

The former
and forthwith, gradual.

Night and day;
watching each gradient,
incremental differences
inch away from the past.

Then and now, swift.

Dusk to dawn;
grey to gold.

today

—

I syphon happiness from the sun,
transmitted through my bloodstream.

lunch break

—

Sure and serene,
overwhelmingly content.

I see the gentle ripple,
river pattern beneath my heels,
lining and meeting the rocks which line,
fifteen feet beneath me,
as my legs sway over them.

Midnight hair,
led against my cheek
from river's wind,
chamomile cools,
while finger pulses
from its contact.

Leaves dangling and
detaching to float along
the river's edge.

I'm soaking up
every second of the moment,
frigid fingers–
nowhere else but here.

Thank you,
for what's here.

For I'm able to live free
and not bound, legs dangling without

temptation to fall forwards,
or to submerge mouth and nose into the
murky river water.

Loving this existence,
loving my King,
loving this ever-mending me,
though His love makes me whole.

This is the moment that I know;
the moment I know that
eternity is only an inch away.

But I'm sitting steadfast in love,
as unrestricted and free flowing
as the exhilaration of
senses within my cells.

The back of my heels bounce
alternately against the
concrete barrier I sit on,
overlooking the river,
the city is my backdrop.

I am fully and wholly alive.

authentic verities
—

Surrounded by incredible love,
just as the sun shines within the day–
as beautiful as the morning's aurora.

More encompassing
than the skin wrapping our bodies,
or the blood within our veins.

More bountiful than the
leaves, needles, buds, blooms.

Steadfast
like the mountains
fastened into the earth.

Just as the east
meets the west,
never ending
yet marrying at every point.

Given to each of us,
and all of us.

—

a f t e r w o r d

Thank you,
for witnessing the small quiver–
that shifted into a quake,
the one that broke dawn
with its shining embrace.

about the author

Regan Noelle Smith is a writer and illustrator based in Pataskala, Ohio.

Regan performs poetry shows and readings across the country. She hosts creative workshops for younger artists–encouraging and inspiring through poetry, creative writing, painting, and illustrating.

She writes within the city, or inside her home with a forest-window view. In the evening, her and her husband enjoy conversation as they walk wherever their feet may land, and watch westwards towards dusk's smooth settle.

Website: *regannoellesmith.com*
Instagram: *@regannoellesmith*

Made in United States
North Haven, CT
06 July 2022

21002896R00114